Romans, Saxons & Vikings

Beliefs and Myths of Roman Britain

Martyn Whittock

Heinemann

First published in Great Britain by
Heinemann Library,
Halley Court, Jordan Hill, Oxford OX2 8EJ
a division of Reed Educational & Professional Publishing Ltd.

OXFORD FLORENCE PRAGUE MADRID
ATHENS MELBOURNE AUCKLAND
KUALA LUMPUR SINGAPORE TOKYO
IBADAN NAIROBI KAMPALA
JOHANNESBURG GABORONE
PORTSMOUTH NH (USA) CHICAGO
MEXICO CITY SAO PAULO

Designed by Ken Vail Graphic Design

Produced by Celia Floyd

Illustrations by Jeff Edwards and Douglas Hall

Originated by Magnet Harlequin Group

Printed in Great Britain by
Bath Press Colourbooks, Glasgow

01 00 99 98 97

10 9 8 7 6 5 4 3 2 1

ISBN 0 431 05976 4

British Library Cataloguing in Publication Data

Whittock, Martyn J. (Martyn John)
Beliefs and myths of Roman Britain
1.Mythology, Roman – Juvenile literature
2.Mythology, British – Juvenile literature
3.Legends – Great Britain – Juvenile literature
I.Title II.Roman Britain
398'.0941

Acknowledgements

The Publishers would like to thank the
following for permission to reproduce
photographs.

Bath Archaeological Trust: p.5;
○ British Museum: pp.4, 5, 6, 11, 12,
14, 21, 24, 25, 27; ○ Corineum Mus.,
Cirencester/John Gibbons Studio: p.23;
○ Robert Estall: p.17; ○ English Heritage
p.19; ○ Museum of London: p.16;
○ Mus. of London Archaeology Unit:
p.29; ○ National Museum of Scotland
1997: pp.9 and 12

Cover photograph shows a detail from
the Corbridge Lanx, and is reproduced
with permission of the British Museum

Our thanks to Dr Stephen Ridd and
Jane Bircher of the Roman Baths
Museum, Bath for their comments
in the preparation of this book.

We would like to thank the
following Wiltshire schools for
valuable comments made regarding
the content and layout of this series:
Fitzmaurice Primary School, Bradford-
on-Avon; Dauntsey's Primary School,
West Lavington; Studley Green
Primary School, Trowbridge.

Details of written sources

S. Ireland, *Roman Britain – a Sourcebook*
Croom Helm 1986: pp.7B, 18C.

Unless the author is named, all other
quotations are from Collingford and
Wright, *The Roman Inscriptions of Britai*
Oxford 1965.

Every effort has been made to contact
copyright holders of any material
reproduced in this book. Any omissions
will be rectified in subsequent printings
if notice is given to the Publisher.

For Andrew, Alastair and Peter.

Contents

Clues about Roman beliefs

The Romans ruled Britain from AD43 until AD410. Many kinds of clues survive from Roman Britain to tell us about people's religious beliefs.

Some of these clues are statues of gods and goddesses, gravestones, things buried with dead people, religious buildings and things used in **worship**.

But we have to be careful how we use these clues. There were different beliefs in different parts of Britain. Religious beliefs changed over time. The Romans brought new religious beliefs to Britain. It can sometimes be hard to tell these new beliefs from things British people believed before the Romans came. Later, many people believed in another new religion – Christianity. Also, many carvings on stone are hard to date. We often cannot tell when they were made.

Source A

They make large figures out of woven branches and fill them with living men. They are then set on fire and the men are killed, burnt by the flames.

A Roman, Julius Caesar, wrote this in about 50BC. He was describing people living in Gaul (modern France). Some historians think similar things happened in Britain.

Source B

A statue of a god worshipped in Roman Britain. It comes from Lincolnshire. It is hard to tell which god it is supposed to be. It looks like Mars, the Roman god of war, but Mars is not usually shown on a horse.

Source C

Objects thrown into a holy spring in the Roman temple at Aquae Sulis (Bath). No-one knows what the mask was used for. We do not know why people put these things into the water.

Source D

A silver dish from Corbridge, Northumberland. It is from a place where the Roman god Apollo was worshipped. But it was found with things that were Christian. Some people may have believed in different religions at the same time! It was probably made in about AD350.

The gods of Rome

The Romans believed in many different gods and goddesses. When they made Britain part of the Roman Empire they brought these Roman beliefs to Britain.

Some of the chief gods and goddesses of Rome:

- Jupiter, the sky-god, the chief god
- Juno, the sister and wife of Jupiter
- Minerva, goddess of wisdom and war
- Mercury, god of trade
- Mars, god of war
- Vulcan, god of fire and blacksmiths
- Diana, goddess of wild animals and of hunting
- Apollo, god of music and medicine
- Neptune, god of the sea
- Silvanus, god of the countryside.
- Vesta, goddess of homes

The Roman army **worshipped** Jupiter above all the other gods.

The god-Emperors

Romans also worshipped their dead **Emperors**. A great temple to the Emperor Claudius was built at Camulodunum (Colchester).

Source A

A jug from Lincoln. On it is written, in Latin: 'I give this to the god Mercury.'

To Jupiter, greatest and best and to the god-Emperor, the 1st cohort of Spaniards set this up.

*Words from a Roman army **altar** found at Maryport, Cumbria. A cohort was a group of soldiers.*

Good luck to the genius (spirit) of this place. Young slave use to your good fortune this goldsmith's shop.

Words carved on an altar placed in a shop. It was found at Malton, Yorkshire.

Rome and British gods

The British people worshipped many different gods and goddesses before the Romans arrived. The Romans were happy to let them carry on doing this. All the Romans demanded was an end to human **sacrifice**. The British and their new rulers worshipped both the Roman and British gods.

Spirits of the land and home

Romans also believed that every place had a spirit living there. In **Latin** each was called a 'genius loci'. This means 'spirit of the place'. Romans also believed that spirits guarded each home.

How do we know?

Sources A and B show us that Roman gods, such as Mercury and Jupiter, were worshipped in Britain.

Source A shows that people gave gifts to the gods. Source B shows that Jupiter was especially important to Roman soldiers. His title shows that they believed he was the greatest and best of the gods.

Source C shows that some people in Roman Britain also believed that each place had a spirit living in it. Here, it was the spirit thought to live in a shop.

The gods of Britain

Before Britain became part of the Roman Empire, people here worshipped many British gods and goddesses. They still did this after Britain became part of the Empire.

However, the Romans killed some British religious leaders. These were the **Druids**. They had opposed the Romans. Their religion included human **sacrifice**.

Local gods and goddesses

Different gods and goddesses were **worshipped** in different parts of Britain. This was because each British **tribe** believed in its own gods.

Sulis was the goddess of the hot springs at Bath. The goddess Brigantia took special care of the Brigantes tribe, who lived in the north of England. Other tribes worshipped other gods.

British and Roman gods

After Britain became part of the **Empire**, many of the British gods and goddesses were linked with Roman gods or goddesses. This was because they were similar in some way.

The goddesses Sulis and Brigantia were like Minerva. A British god, called Cocidius, was like the Roman god Mars. British and Roman gods and goddesses were sometimes worshipped together.

Source A

To the Italian, German, Gallic and British mother goddesses. Antonius Lucretianus, who has been given special duties by the **provincial governor**, restored this altar.

Words on a Roman altar. The altar was found at Winchester, Hampshire.

Source B

To the holy god Cocidius. Quintus Peltrasius Maximus willingly and rightly fulfilled his vow.

Words from a Roman altar, found at Bewcastle, Cumbria.

Source C

To the god Mars Cocidius,the holy. Aelius Vitalianus willingly and rightly gave this as a gift.

Words from an altar. It was found at Bewcastle, Cumbria.

Source D

A carving of the British goddess Brigantia. She is holding a spear, like the Roman goddess Minerva.

How do we know?

Source A shows that some people in Roman Britain tried to make sure they did not miss out a god or goddess when they built an altar. This one includes lots of goddesses, from different places.

Source B shows that one of the British gods was called Cocidius. Source C shows that this god was linked to the Roman god Mars. Both were probably war-gods.

Source D shows that Brigantia was made to look like the Roman goddess Minerva.

New ideas from the East

While Britain was part of the Roman Empire new religious ideas spread across the Empire. Many of these new ideas came from the Middle East.

In time these new ideas reached Britain. They were probably brought by Roman soldiers and merchants.

Beliefs from Syria

One goddess was called the Syrian goddess. She was **worshipped** at the fort at Carvoran, Northumberland. Some soldiers from Syria lived at this fort, and they probably brought this belief with them.

Another goddess was Astarte, who was thought to make things grow. She was worshipped with a god called Heracles. He was first worshipped in Greece.

Another Syrian goddess was Cybele, goddess of the land. She was worshipped with the Syrian god Attis.

Beliefs from Egypt

At York the Egyptian god Serapis was worshipped. A goddess called Isis was worshipped in London. At Rochester, in Kent, there was a **shrine** to the god Osiris.

Source A

To the holy god Serapis. Claudius Hieronymianus, of the Sixth Legion, built this temple.

Words carved on stone and found at York. Claudius had been an important Roman official in the Middle East. Then he was moved to Britain.

Source B

To Heracles of Tyre. Diodora the priestess set this up.

Words from an altar. It was found at Corbridge, Northumberland. They were written in Greek. Tyre is in the Middle East.

Beliefs from Persia

A Persian god, named Mithras, was popular with soldiers. He was a god of light, and was often worshipped with the Roman sun-god, Apollo.

Christianity

The belief in Jesus as the Son of God also started in the Middle East. By AD200 there were Christians in Britain too.

How do we know?

The sources show beliefs from the Middle East were found in Britain.

Source A shows Serapis was worshipped at York. Source B shows Heracles was worshipped at Corbridge. Source C shows a Syrian goddess was worshipped at Carvoran. Source D shows that Egyptian gods were worshipped in London.

Ideas and languages travelled with people. This is shown in Sources A and B. Source B is in Greek, which was spoken in the east of the Empire.

Source C

She is mother of the gods, the Syrian goddess. She weighs life and laws in her balance.

Words from an altar. It was found at Carvoran, Northumberland.

Source D

A statue of the Egyptian god Harpocrates, son of Isis and Osiris. This was found in London.

Temples of the gods

In Roman Britain temples were built. These were places where a god or goddess was worshipped.

Large temples

Some temples were very large. A great temple was built at Camulodunum (Colchester). The Emperor was **worshipped** there. Another great temple was built at 'Aquae Sulis' (Bath). Here the goddesses Sulis and Minerva were worshipped. They were thought to be the same goddess. There were only a few large temples like these.

Smaller temples

Most temples were small. The statue of a god was kept there. Around this was an area surrounded by a wall.

In this area people buried gifts they wanted to give to the god. These were sometimes pots, coins or jewellery. Sometimes they were parts of animals, which had been **sacrificed** to the god. Many of these temples were built where different gods had been worshipped before Romans came to Britain. They were mainly in the south and east, as can be seen from the map.

Source A

A special head-dress worn by a priest. This was found at Stony Stratford, in Buckinghamshire.

Worn like this?

12

Source B

A carving of a Roman sacrifice to the gods. It comes from Bridgeness, Scotland. An army officer pours drink on an altar. Animals are ready to be sacrificed. Music is being played.

Places where small temples were built in Roman Britain

How do we know?

Source A shows that priests sometimes wore special head-dresses.

Source B shows how sacrifices were carried out. Animals were killed. Drink was poured on an altar. Music was played.

What happened at temples?

Animals were often killed to please the gods. The idea was that, in return, the god would look after the people who gave the sacrifice.

A priest called a haruspex might look at the animal's insides, in order to foretell the future. Some priests wore special head-dresses to show they were important people.

Sometimes drink was poured on an **altar** to honour the gods. Music was sometimes played to please the gods.

13

Private prayers and promises

Most people in Roman Britain did not go in a large group to worship their gods. They did so on their own, or with a few friends and family. Many did not even go to temples to do this.

Prayers in the home

People believed that gods and goddesses looked after their homes. Many homes had a special place where a small statue of a god was placed. This place was called a lararium. These places, where a god was thought to live, are also called **shrines**.

The little statues of gods were often made of bronze. Members of the family paid for them to be made. As well as gods, the spirits of dead members of the family were also **worshipped** at home.

Sometimes little shrines were made of lead. They had doors and the figure of a god inside. They could be carried from place to place. One from Wallsend, Northumberland, had a figure of Mercury inside. One from Wroxeter, Shropshire, had a figure of Venus inside.

Source A

A little bronze statue of Mars. It was found in Lincolnshire. Writing on it says it was paid for by two brothers, Bruccius and Caratius.

Altars in the countryside

There were very few temples in the north of Roman Britain. But here many more little **altars** have been found.

These were specially made out of stone. Words on them usually thanked a god or goddess for doing something. The person who thought the god might help them, or had helped them, paid for the altar. Sacrifices were made on the altar.

Most of these altars were put up by people in the army. They were ways in which a person could show they worshipped a particular god. They hoped that doing this would make sure the god went on helping them.

Source B

To the god Hercules. Keep the person well who put this up. And look after his fellow soldiers. Put up after the slaughter of a band of **barbarians** by the cavalry regiment called 'Augusta', because it is so brave.

Words carved on stone, from Carlisle, Cumbria. Augusta means brave.

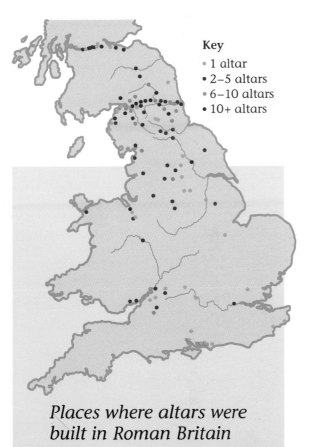

Key
- 1 altar
- 2–5 altars
- 6–10 altars
- 10+ altars

Places where altars were built in Roman Britain

How do we know?

Source A shows the kind of statue placed in a lararium. It was paid for by a family.

Source B shows the kinds of words carved on altars. They usually thanked a god for doing something. Or they asked for something. Here the god is thanked for a victory over enemy **tribes**. He is asked to keep the soldiers safe.

Secret places, a secret god

Some people in Roman Britain had very secret beliefs. They only shared them with other people who believed in their god.

Mystery religions

The most secret groups of people were part of what are called Mystery Religions. People could only join these groups after going through secret **ceremonies**. The people who believed in the gods of the Mystery Religions met together privately. Other people could not share in their **worship**.

Mithras

One of the Mystery Religions involved the worship of Mithras. This god came from Persia, in the Middle East. Mithras became popular amongst soldiers in Britain after about AD200.

Followers of Mithras believed he was god of light and the sun, the enemy of evil and darkness. He was often pictured killing a bull. His followers thought that life on earth had come from the blood of this bull. Mithras had a helper named Cautopates. This kind of story about a god is called a **myth**, or legend.

Source A

To the god Mithras.
To Cautopates.
To the invincible sun-god.

Words carved on an altar found at Lanchester, County Durham.

Source B

A carving of Mithras killing a bull. From a temple in London, built about AD240.

Temple of Mithras, Carrawburgh, Northumberland. Built in about AD220

How do we know?

Source A shows that Mithras was thought to be the god of the sun. Cautopates was a helper of the god.

Source B shows one of the main beliefs about Mithras. He triumphed over evil by killing a magical bull.

Source C shows how small temples of Mithras could be. They had altars and carvings at the front. On each side of the room were places to sit or stand.

Becoming a follower of Mithras

To become a follower, people had to go through frightening or painful experiences. These often involved the use of fire and water. Often people had to fast. This means going without food.

The temples of Mithras

Temples of Mithras were small. They were not made to hold lots of people. Altars and carvings were often put at one end. Worshippers sat on either side of a central aisle.

Behind a curtain was a private room. Sometimes it held a pit, with a fire beside it. This was where people who wanted to join the religion went through secret ceremonies.

Old beliefs and magic

The Romans brought many changes to the beliefs of British people. But some things did not change. Also, some people tried to use magic.

Changes and old beliefs

The Romans changed the way gods were **worshipped** in Britain. They brought new gods to worship. They brought the idea of making stone statues of gods and stone **altars** for them. Building temples out of stone was another new idea.

Some British ideas about the gods stayed the same though. Many people carried on worshipping gods in the way they had before the Romans came. These people did not build altars, or temples. We do not know the names of the gods they worshipped.

At Shiptonthorpe, east Yorkshire, people thought the pond where they got water for their village was special. They buried pots, skulls and young animals and human babies there. In many places coins, pots and little statues were thrown into wells. Things like this had happened before the Romans came and continued while Britain was part of the **Empire**. These beliefs were not Roman ideas about religion.

Source A

Britain today is keen on magic and does it with a lot of **ceremony**.

A Roman, Pliny the Elder, wrote this. He died in AD79.

Source B

The soldier was told in a dream to get Fabius's wife to set up this altar, to the nymphs who are to be worshipped.

Carved on stone by a spring at Risingham, Northumberland.

Source C

I curse Tretia Maria. May her life and mind and memory and liver and lungs be mixed together. May she be unable to speak what is secret.

Carved on lead and found in London.

18

Source D

A little model of a dog thrown into a sacred well along Hadrian's Wall.

How do we know?

Source A shows us some people living in Britain tried to use magic to change their lives. Source C shows some people tried to use magic to harm their enemies.

Sources B and D show people thought spirits lived in water. They had believed this before the Romans came. Even though a Roman altar was used in Source B, these were really old beliefs. The Romans called the spirits of the water 'nymphs', because this was the name given to water spirits in their own religion.

Magic

Some people tried to protect themselves by wearing special necklaces, or carrying special objects. These are called lucky **charms**. Some had words written on them in the Greek and Hebrew languages. Some were possibly used as magic spells.

Some people tried to make magic to hurt other people. **Curses** were written on sheets of lead. These were placed in a temple. Some were thrown into water. Some people also thought that spirits called nymphs lived in water and would help people, if asked properly.

The coming of Christianity

One of the beliefs that came from the east of the Empire was Christianity. No-one is sure when the first Christians arrived in Britain. There are not a lot of clues that have survived to tell us.

Christians believed (and still believe) that Jesus Christ is the Son of God, who was killed and was brought back to life again. He died in about AD33. Christians think that if you believe in Jesus, you can have life after death, with God.

This belief started in the east of the Roman **Empire**. It is an important part of Christian beliefs to share the Gospel (good news) about Jesus. Early Christians spread their beliefs across the Roman Empire.

Christianity reaches Britain

Christian beliefs were probably brought to Britain by merchants and soldiers. There were groups of Christians living in some of the towns of Roman Britain by AD314. They were well organised. They had their own leaders, called bishops.

Source A

There are places in Britain, which the Romans have never reached, which believe in Christ.

The Christian writer Tertullian wrote this shortly before AD200. He lived in north Africa.

Source B

Eborius, bishop of the city of York in the **province** of Britain. Restitutus, bishop of London. Adelphius, bishop of the city Colonia Londenensium.

A list of British Christian leaders, AD314.

A silver plate from Risley Park, in Derbyshire. The pictures are not Christian. But words on it show it was given to 'the Bogiensian church'. No-one knows where this church was.

Clues from the first Christians

Some silver spoons, ornaments and plates have the first two letters of Christ's name on them. This was a Christian badge. Some villas had Christian pictures on the walls. Some had Christian **mosaics** on the floor.

Sometimes non-Christian silver plates were used by Christians. The pictures on them were not always Christian but they put Christian words on them.

There are not a lot of these clues. Christians did not build rich temples, or bury treasure in the ground, or put it in water, like the people who believed in Roman gods. They did not make lots of statues of Jesus.

How do we know?

Source B shows Christian beliefs had spread to Britain by AD314. Source A shows they might have been here for a long time. But this writer did not come from Britain. We do not know how much he knew.

Source C shows that non-Christian things were sometimes used by the early Christians.

Trouble between the old and new beliefs

Christians were sometimes killed by the Roman rulers. There was sometimes trouble between people who believed in the old gods and those who believed in Jesus.

Romans allowed people to **worship** their own gods. This was as long as they also worshipped the Roman gods. Christians would not worship Roman gods. Christians would not worship the **Emperor**. They thought there was only one God. This was the Christian God.

Christians in trouble

Roman rulers sometimes punished Christians for not worshipping Roman gods. One British Christian was killed at the town of Verulamium, in about AD209. His name was Alban. This place is now called St Albans. Other British Christians also died. Two were killed at Caerleon, in Wales. They were Aaron and Julius. This was probably in about AD257.

These attacks on Christians ended in AD311. In AD313 the new Roman Emperor, Constantine, began to support the Christian church.

Source A

To stop Britain being plunged into darkness, God lit the bright lights of the holy **martyrs**. I mean St Alban at Verulamium, together with Aaron and Julius, **citizens** of the City of the Legions.

A British Christian wrote this. His name was Gildas. He may have written it as early as about AD500.

Source B

This holy spot, wrecked by insolent hands was cleaned afresh by Gaius Severius Emeritus, centurion in charge of the region.

Carved on stone and found at Bath. This altar to the old gods may have been wrecked by Christians after about AD320.

Source C

The base of a stone column, put up to worship the god Jupiter. It is from Cirencester (Glos).

Writing on it says it was 'restored'. This probably means someone had earlier tried to destroy it.

Conflict with old beliefs

After about AD320 some temples of the old Roman gods were destroyed in Britain. They may have been destroyed by Christians. The Christians called people who believed in the old gods **pagans**.

In AD360 a new Roman Emperor, Julian, tried to make everyone in the Empire worship the old gods. He failed. But in Britain some people tried to revive the old temples for a time. New temples were built at Maiden Castle (Dorset) and at Uley (Glos.) The one at Uley was later smashed. Its statue of Mercury was broken up and buried. A Christian church was put up to replace it. We do not know how many Christians there were in Roman Britain. In country areas some people carried on with the old pagan beliefs.

How do we know?

Source A tells us the names of some Christians killed in Britain. The City of the Legions was probably Caerleon, in Wales. Gildas wrote a long time afterwards but other writers also mentioned Alban. So it seems to have happened as Gildas said it did.

Sources B and C show that some of the things made to worship the old gods of Rome were broken. But we cannot be sure the damage was done by Christians.

23

Finding the first Christian churches

It is not easy to find the first churches. Early Christians did not build big buildings in Britain.

The first Christians met together to **worship** God. They met together in churches. For many years Christians had been badly treated by Roman rulers. So they met together quietly, in small places.

Churches in country homes?

Christians may have met to worship in each other's homes. Some Roman villas, in the country, had Christian signs painted on their walls, or set in **mosaics** on the floor. Some had pictures painted on the walls, showing people praying the way Roman Christians did. These may have been places where Christians met together.

Lead tanks have been found. They might have held water to **baptise** people in. One at Icklingham, Suffolk, had a Christian sign on it. This sign was the first two letters of Christ's name.

Source A

A mosaic from Hinton St Mary villa, Dorset. The sign behind the person's head is a Christian one. It is the first two letters of Christ's name, in Greek. It is from about AD350.

Source B

A painting from the wall of Lullingstone villa, Kent. It shows people praying like Roman Christians. It is from about AD350.

How do we know?

Source A is probably a picture of Jesus Christ. The sign stands for his name. This may mean that Christians met in this villa to worship God.

Source B might have been from a Christian church. It shows Christians praying. Pictures of people praying like this have been found in other parts of the **Empire**. This may mean there was a little church at this villa.

Key

- Villa with Christian pictures
- Possible church
- Tanks which may have been used to baptise people in

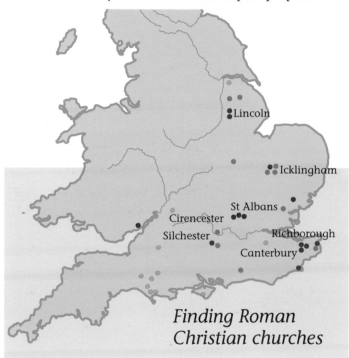

Finding Roman Christian churches

Churches in towns?

Many Christians lived in towns. Buildings which might have been churches have been found in a number of Roman towns. But it is hard to be sure. Early churches were not built in one special way. Older buildings were sometimes changed into churches. It is hard to tell if a building was used as a church.

25

Places of the dead

From about AD43 until about AD200, the bodies of most dead people were burnt. This is called cremation.

For about 150 years after Britain became part of the Roman **Empire** most people were cremated. We do not know why people chose to do this. Perhaps they believed that burning the bodies of dead people freed their spirits.

Cemeteries

Places where dead people are buried are called cemeteries. Roman laws said that all cemeteries should be outside settlements. Most Roman cemeteries were placed along the roads leading out of towns.

Boxes, jars and pots

The burnt ashes of cremated people were put in different containers for burial. Some were put in pots. Some pots had faces decorating the outside. Sometimes ashes were put in glass jars. Sometimes they were put in wooden boxes.

Source A

No one may bring, burn or bury a dead body within the boundary of the town. No new place to burn bodies may be set up within half a mile of the town.

A Roman law about where to burn and bury the dead. It was a law for the town of Urso in Spain. It was made by Julius Caesar in the first century BC. The same rules were followed in Britain.

A special pot called a face-pot. It was used to bury the ashes of a dead person. Several pots like this have been found around the Roman town of Camulodunum (Colchester, Essex).

How do we know?

Source A shows that Roman laws were strict about where cemeteries could be placed. They had to go outside settlements. These laws were followed throughout the Empire.

Source B shows that pots were sometimes used to bury ashes in. Sometimes these were pots with special decorations on them. Face-pots were popular in one part of Roman Britain.

We do not know if the face was meant to mean something. It might have been a god. It might have been the dead person. We cannot tell.

Grave goods

Often things were buried with the ashes. People seem to have thought that things buried with people could be used by their spirits in the next world. These included money, jewellery, food.

The money was probably meant to pay the spirit who took dead people across the river Styx to the world of the dead. His name was Charon.

It was a long journey to the place of the dead. Food may have been to eat on the way. Shoes were buried, too. They may also have been to use on the journey.

Changing ideas about death

At first most people in Roman Britain burnt dead bodies, then buried them. Later, they buried them without burning them first. Christians liked this idea too.

After about AD200 more and more people buried their dead without burning them first. Soon almost everyone did this. No-one knows why this change happened. Most of the bodies were buried with things to be used in the next life.

Coffins of wood, stone and lead

Many dead people were buried in special boxes. These are called coffins. Richer families paid for stone or lead coffins. Poorer people had wooden coffins. The poorest people had no coffins at all.

Preserving bodies

Sometimes the coffins were filled with something called gypsum. This went hard around a body. It sometimes stopped a body from rotting away. Perhaps it was thought people buried like this would have better bodies in the next life.

Source A

A plan of a late Roman cemetery. It is at Poundbury, Dorset. The graves are shown as little rectangles. They are all facing in the same direction.
Archaeologists *think that Christians were probably buried here.*

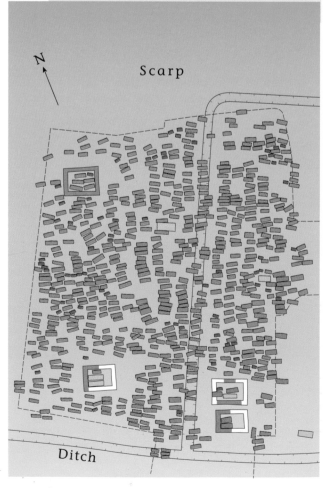

Key

⬜ Building around graves

▬ Stone coffin

▬ Lead-lined coffin

▬ Grave or wooden coffin

▪ Child's grave

Source B

Burials from London. The coffins were filled with gypsum.

How do we know?

Source A shows that Christian cemeteries often had graves facing in the same direction. They faced from east to west. But some Romans had started doing this before Christianity became popular. So the people buried this way might not all have been Christians.

Source B shows that some Romans tried to preserve dead bodies. But we cannot be sure of why they did this.

Christian ideas about death

Roman Christians believed that people could not take objects into the next life. They usually did not bury things with the dead. They did not burn bodies. They buried people with their heads pointing west. They thought a day would come when God would give them new life in heaven. When they stood up they would be facing east. This was the direction of Jerusalem – a holy city to Christians.

But Christians may not have started this idea about the direction of graves. Some people were already doing this before Christian beliefs became popular. So Christians may have been doing something which some **pagans** also thought was a good idea.

Glossary

altar a carved stone on which sacrifices were made to Roman gods

archaeologists people who dig up and study things made in the past

baptise people are baptised with water when they join the Christian Church

barbarians tribes from outside the Roman Empire

ceremonies doing something important in a special way

charms objects supposed to keep the owner safe, by magic

citizens members of the Roman Empire, who were protected by its laws

curse magic supposed to cause harm to another person

Druids priests in the British religion. They carried out human sacrifices.

Empire the large area of land ruled by the Romans. It covered parts of Europe, North Africa and the Middle East. The ruler was called the **Emperor**.

governor the person in charge of the running of Roman Britain. He was given the job by the Emperor.

Latin the official language of the Roman Empire

martyrs Christians who die for their beliefs

mosaic a patterned floor made from pieces of stone

myth a story about the gods, or imaginary people to explain things about the world. Also called a legend.

pagans followers of a non-Christian religion

province a part of the Roman Empire

sacrifice giving something to the pagan gods, often an animal's life

shrine a special place which is thought to be holy

tribe a group of people often related to each other, having a similar way of life and the same leaders. Many tribes were conquered by the Romans.

worship praising and showing respect for God, or the gods. It may involve singing, praying, doing things in a special way.

Timeline – Romans, Anglo-Saxons and Vikings

Roman Age	
AD1	
AD100	
AD200	
AD300	
AD400	
AD500	
AD600	
AD700	
AD800	
AD900	
AD1000	
AD1100	

AD1		
	AD43	Romans invade Britain
		Pliny the Elder writes about magic in Britain
		Temple of the god-Emperor Claudius built at Colchester
		Most dead bodies burnt, then buried
AD100		
		People start burying dead bodies without burning them first
		Tertullian writes about Christians in Britain
AD200		
	AD240	Temple of Mithras built in London.
		Alban, Aaron and Julius killed for being Christians
AD300		
	AD313	Emperor Constantine joins the Christians
	AD360	Emperor Julian opposes Christianity – he fails
		New pagan temple built at Uley
		Uley pagan temple destroyed. Replaced by a Christian church.
AD400		
	AD410	Britain stops being part of the Roman Empire

Index

Numbers in plain type (7) refer to the text. Numbers in italic type (*5*) refer to a caption.